MW00908339

FINISH LINE

Thoughts to guide you on your way

by John Dmytryszyn

Finish Line

Thoughts to guide you on your way

Website: Outstandinglife.net
Email address: johnnyd@outstandinglife.net

P.O. Box 1049
Southgate MI 48195
Phone 1-800-792-3229 or 1-734-556-3001

ISBN - 0-9710964-7-3

2 ←─────────────────────────────────

Credits

Front cover photograph by Damir Frkovic / Masterfile

Layout and design: Alpha 21 Graphics Center
                   22400 Telegraph Road
                   Southfield MI 48034

"Today You Hurt Me" written by Nicole Kozub

"Bullies" written by Jessa Dmytryszyn

A special thanks to my friend, Dr. A. Anne Bowers, Jr. for her expertise and assistance with the final touches and polishing with my thoughts.

Thank you to my good friend Scott Witz for being there for me throughout this whole project. I couldn't have done it without your assistance and hard work.

4 ⟵

Table of Contents

Never-Ever 11
Life is Tough 12
Make It Happen 13
Babe Ruth 14
Today .15
Today You Hurt Me 16-17
Blaming Society 18
Life is Like a Puzzle 19
Biggest Man–Smallest Child 20
Don't Be Afraid 21
Image .22
Wayne Gretsky 23
Spring Time 24
When You're Young 25
Hitch a Ride 26
If not You 27
For You 28
Obstacles 29
Living the "Outstanding" Life . .30
Hit the Road 31
Procrastination 32
Two Types of People 33
Ladders of Success 34
Focus Power 35
A successful Career 36
Things You Regret 37
Being a Champion 38
Disappointment 39
Reality .40
Get a Hand Up 41
Love 42
Looking for Love 43
The Simple Things 44
Alarm Bells 45
Positive Attitude 46
Reach .47

Without Goals 48
Window Shopping 49
Trust 50
Memorial Day 51
Outstanding Day 52
Wardrobe of Vocabulary 53
Clear Focus and Clear Vision . .54
The Longer I Live 55
Understanding Courage 56
Just 57
Outstanding People 58
Image .59
Focus .60
Who are Winners? 61
Time 62
Change 63
Not Always Right 64
Best Example 65
Destination 66
Anchors 67
Win 68
Commitment 69
Cracker Jack Box 70
Think a Minute 71
But 72
What If? 73
Dare? .74
Tough Quality 75
Sky's the Limit 76
Greatness 77
News Flash 78
Bullies .79
Pressure 80
21 Ways to Live
    The Outstanding Life 81

Dedication

Dedicated to my Grandpa Hornok who inspired me and helped me find the best within myself. And to my daughter, Jessa, whom I love with all my heart. Thank you for your motivation. It is through both, that all of my dreams have been kept alive.

8 ←—————————————————————

Introduction

How many times have you gotten to the end of the road and asked yourself, "Do I go left or right?" I look back and see all the choices I made that brought me to where I am today. This book is written about those choices and events in my life, people I've learned from, and people who have inspired me.

People often ask me, "How did you get started?" I don't think there really is a starting point, just choices that bring you to your own "Finish Line." We've all come to that point in the road where we have to make the decision to go left or right. My decisions started at a very young age. I was held back in 2nd grade when my teacher told my parents that I couldn't read or communicate well. I think it was in the 4th grade that my teacher once again told my parents that I wouldn't amount to much. What if I had gone down the road that those people had chosen for me? Thank God I'll never know. With the help of my family, I chose to believe in myself.

After high school my career path took me in many directions, from a small business owner, to the marketing director of a Fortune 500 company. I was married at 23, divorced at 24 with a beautiful baby girl. Throughout all of this, I crossed the paths of many lives, and I started to receive letters from people that wanted to thank me for inspiring them. As I looked back on my yearbooks and the things people wrote, I realized they were writing the same kind of sentiments. Finally it hit me. This was my gift to give back to the world. Six years ago I reached that road sign that gave me the choice to go left or right. Two weeks before Christmas I quit my job and decided to share my gift with the world.

As for this particular book, I wanted 4th graders to be able to read it and get something out of it, as well as their parents when they read the same thought. The struggles and challenges that children face are just as confusing as the ones that adults face. Hopefully this book will provide you with some thoughts and tools for making the decisions you need to make.

Just remember: The "Finish Line" is also the Starting Line.

FINISH LINE

Never-Ever

Never ever listen to anyone who tells you
something can't be done.

People who think about failure
will generally succeed at failing;
Their minds are already thinking about failure.

But people who think about solutions,
rather than road blocks,
will always reach the finish line before anyone else!

Life is Tough

Life is tough sometimes.

There are a million decisions to make,
and none of them are easy.

There are things you want to do, but can't,
and things you don't want to do, but must.

There are good times and hard times,
and days you feel like nobody understands
what it is like to be you…

and you are probably right.

Today go out of your way to be nice to someone;
they may be having a bad day.

So, no matter how tough things get,
just be OUTSTANDING!

Make It Happen

Let me start by asking you some questions.

1. What dreams or goals would you have
   if money was no problem?

2. What plans would you make
   if you knew you could make it happen?

3. What projects would you launch
   if you had the wisdom to solve any problem
   and the power to get rid of all the obstacles?

The secret can be summarized in 4C's.

They are:
  • **Curiosity**
  • **Confidence**
  • **Courage**
  • **Consistency.**

The most important is **Confidence.**

Remember,

anybody can dream,

anybody can plan,

but not everybody

      can make it happen.

Babe Ruth

Today most people are worried about themselves
and not their team.

Babe Ruth is one of the top home run hitters
in the world.

He never struck out as much as today's sluggers
because he realized
the team's success
was more important
than *individual statistics.*

Today

Today is tomorrow.

Tomorrow is today.

But tomorrow is promised to no one.

I'll live for today.

What day will you live for?

Today You Hurt Me

Today you hurt me, did you know?
I begged and cried for you not to go,
I looked away as you closed the door,
What are you so angry for?
Is it something I did,
Or something I said?
When I smiled at you, you just turned your head.

Today you hurt me, as you closed me out.
You don't even know what my life is about.
I try to be happy.
I try to stay strong.
What you're doing seems so wrong.
I try to come close,
But you push me away.
You really hurt me again today.

Today you hurt me, as I remembered the past.
The bottle came first,
And I often came last.
Growing up in a home with no one to care,
No one to talk to
No one was there.

Today you hurt me, I felt so scared.
For this journey, I am prepared;
Prepared for the sadness,
Prepared for the pain,
No matter what,
My love will remain.
It lives in your heart,
And runs deep inside.
It will always be there,
Please don't hide.

Today you hurt me, though I'm feeling quite strong,
The days awaiting will be long.
I will use my strength to get me through,
I will take my time,
And be patient with you.
Because it is an illness,
You have no control.
It runs through your blood,
Then takes over your soul.

Today you hurt me, but I will forgive,
I don't condone the way that you live,
You've made hard choices,
You have sacrificed,
You are the one who has given me life.
I'll forget the pain,
I'll forget the sorrow,

Please, don't hurt me tomorrow.

Blaming Society

People are quick to blame society
for its problems or their failure,

But the fact of the matter is
that everyone is responsible for their own lives.

The biggest obstacles you ever face, you create.

Don't limit your options or sell yourself short.

After all, if you don't believe in yourself,
How can you expect anyone else
to believe in you?

Life is Like a Puzzle

Life is like a puzzle.

You're never sure if or where you fit in.

You sometimes push and squeeze
into places you
really don't belong.

There are days you're ready
to tear all the pieces apart
and begin again.

Sometimes you might think,
"If I were only a different color, size, or shape
then I would know exactly where I belong."

But soon, with lots of patience and love,
You know the pieces will all begin to fall into place,
and lying there before you
will be the beautiful picture
of who you are and
what you have become.

This is John Dmytryszyn telling you
to help somebody put their puzzle together.

Biggest Man–Smallest Child

You can be the biggest man
or the smallest child,

Everyone likes to be noticed.

Being noticed for doing your job is great,
but being noticed for being yourself
is something special,
something that neither you
nor anyone else
can put a price tag on.

Don't Be Afraid

Don't be afraid
To meet with people
who hold vastly
different views than you.

A variety of opinions
is actually a wealth of knowledge
in disguise.

Image

"Image is nothing!"

"Image is everything!"

They're both wrong!!

Image is something you work for.

It's part show and part go.

If it's all show,
you're just a hotdog!

If it's all go,
you're underestimated!

You must have the talent and the desire
to do the job to the best of your ability,

But don't be afraid
to reap the rewards
of your hard work.

Wayne Gretzky

Wayne Gretzky has scored more goals
than anyone
in the history of the NHL!

Who do you think has taken the most shots?
That's right...Wayne Gretzky!

He believed in himself,
he made it happen.

There's only one certainty in life...
You miss 100% of the shots you never take!

Spring Time

Spring is the most positive time of the year.

It's when home owners do major
cleaning and repairing.

Young adults are said to be in the
springtime of their lives.

So everyone's goal should be
to make everyday
another day of spring.

Improve something about yourself
each and everyday...

Starting today!

When You're Young

When you're young,
everyday seems
to last an eternity.

But, as you grow older
the days grow shorter and shorter.

It's difficult to remember details from your childhood,
because as a child
these details seem meaningless.

But it's important never to forget them as an adult,
because as an adult
every moment counts.

This is John Dmytryszyn telling you never to forget
those outstanding memories!

Hitch a Ride

There are many different kinds of people
in the world.

People who know where they want to go,
but don't know how to get there.

People who have no clue where they're going,
but just drive around.

And people who know exactly where they're going,
AND know how to get there!

If you don't fit into this last group,
then you better hitch a ride!!!

If not You...

If not you, then who?

If not here, then where?

If not now, then when?

If not YOU,

Right HERE,

Right NOW,

THEN WHY???

For You

Live each day as if it were your last.

Build on the future and not on the past.

Reach for the stars, but don't fall down.

Get back up with a smile, not a frown.

Dream big, there's no room for small.

No matter what, walk proud and tall.

Don't wait for things to go your way.

Go out and get them, forever to stay.

Never give up and never let go.

Strive to be the best, and then they'll know

You've become the best that you can be.

Believe in yourself, and that's all you need.

Obstacles

Obstacles are seen differently,
depending upon your personality.

Some people see an obstacle
as a mountain to climb,

Others see it as a block wall
with no way over or around.

I don't know about you,
but I have always believed
that a man can climb a mountain
before he can ram his head through a block wall.

Living the "Outstanding" Life

O Out of every situation, the outcome can be a positive or a negative.

U You have the power within yourself to decide what that outcome will be.

T Two negatives make a positive, so why not go straight for the plus.

S Sharing of yourself does not mean taking away, but adding to the whole.

T Thank you for taking the time to ask.

A A dream is reality in the making.

N Never look at past choices as mistakes, only experiences to learn and grow from.

D Dare to live beyond the limitations others have set for you.

I I can make a difference, even if it is only one person at a time.

N Now is the time to stand out, to rise above the rest.

G Go straight to the top; don't settle for the middle.

Hit the Road

You're worth what you think you're worth.

Don't sell yourself short.

Have faith in what you're doing,
because it is the best thing out there.

If they aren't buying,
then don't be afraid to tell them
to "HIT THE ROAD."

Procrastination

Remember that old saying,
"Don't put off until tomorrow
what you can do today"?

That's generally true, but left unchecked,
procrastination becomes laziness,
and laziness is like cancer,
it will slowly kill every organ in your body.

You need to keep both your mind
and body in good shape if you expect them
to perform to the best of their ability.

Two Types of People

There are two types of people in the world…
negative people and positive people.

A negative person will see an obstacle
and say it's impossible.

A positive person will see that same obstacle
and start envisioning a solution.

A negative person sees barriers,
and a positive person finds solutions.

Are you a negative person or a positive person?

I'll bet on the positive person every time.

Ladders of Success

The ladders of success come in all shapes and sizes.

You can't be afraid to climb off the small ladder
to climb onto a bigger one.

Today, it seems that too many people are content
with standing on top
of that small step ladder of success,
while the big ladders of success
go unused.

Right now, I challenge you to step down,
take a deep breath, and start a new climb
on a taller success ladder.

There will always be someone out there
building a taller ladder.

Focus Power

"Danielson" is a famous saying from the movie
Karate Kid.

I still hear people say it to friends who seem
to have an impossible task in front of them.

Now, what is the important meaning of that saying?

Is it Danielson?

I don't know anyone named Danielson...

It's not power either!

After all, unfocused power is just a waste of energy.

Focus is the key.

If you focus on any problem, no matter how difficult,
then the solution will always be in your grasp.

A Successful Career

I would like everyone out there to visualize
a successful career.

I bet most people see piles of money.

But, if money dominates your thoughts,
it will control your mind.

First define a successful career.

Find something that you love to do.

Do it and do it well, and get paid for it!

It could be a minimum wage job
or a six figure income.

Either way, if you are doing
what you love for a living,
then your career is a success.

Things You Regret

The things you regret most in your life
are the things you don't do!

Sure you regret your embarrassments,
everyone does!

But, I would rather die trying than die wondering.

That is the difference
between people who have courage
and people who are afraid.

Being a Champion

A person doesn't have to be the best at something to be a champion.

A champion is a person made up of 3 qualities:

1) An outstanding will to succeed

2) A fight to never give up

3) A satisfaction that they did their very best

A true champion may never win a trophy.

They may never receive an award,
but if they give 110%
to what they are competing for,
they know they are a champion.

Disappointment

Disappointment will come for yourself
and for the ones that you love,
but getting past it and surviving the despair
is achievement.

Most people believe disappointment is failure.

If you allow yourself to live that way,
you deprive yourself
of learning from your mistakes.

After all,
mistakes are made to be
learned from.

Reality

Reality can be blurred by many things,
  –wishful thinking
  –alcohol
  –lack of sleep
  –drugs or dreaming.

Some of these things are from choice,
and others are natural.

Avoid the bad choices
and strive for what nature says reality should be.

In other words,
follow that dream, and don't get caught up
in things that aren't real.

Get a Hand Up

The most pathetic phrase
that I have ever heard in my life
is any two-word phrase
that ends in "me."
Whether it be, "Help me!" or "Save me!"

This is a statement of surrender: "I can't do it!"

After all, if you are sitting there
with your arms crossed,
then how can you grab a hand up?

The hand of opportunity is there,
but you have to grab it!

Love

Never underestimate the power of love.

Its strength can take you to the top of a mountain
or the bottom of a pit.

When your love is at its peak,
so are your ambitions.
But when your love is in the pit,
so are your feelings.

So keep your love strong,
because it is the fuel
that keeps you going.

Looking for Love

80% of songs are written about love ...
either finding love,
losing love,
or looking for love.

Everyone is looking for love,
but most people don't look in the right place.

The first place you should look is in a mirror.

If that person doesn't love you,
then you cannot expect anyone else to.

So, tell that person in the mirror that you love him,
and mean it!!

The Simple Things

What makes you happy are the simple things in life!

They are also the hardest to find.

We are all on a search in life,
but some people have a map.

If you don't own a map,
then don't be afraid to stop
and ask for directions.

Alarm Bells

All animals have defense mechanisms.

Some birds will fake a broken wing
to lead a predator away from their nest,
and everyone knows
what a skunk uses for its defense.

When you develop a positive attitude,
you will develop a defense mechanism
against negative thoughts.

An alarm bell will sound in your head
when you are around someone
who is negative.

It could be
    10 minutes
      5 minutes
        5 seconds,
but you have to get out of there fast,
so you are able to keep your thoughts positive.

Positive Attitude

Having a positive attitude in life is important,
but not essential.

Never apologize for having a positive attitude,
but don't do or say anything
you should apologize for
if you have a negative attitude
that day.

Reach

A tree doesn't reach its full potential
until it is cut down.

Whether it is used for lumber
to build a home,
a piece of furniture,
or used to transmit news.

So don't cry when a tree is cut down,
because most advances in life
start with a small
                  step
        backwards.

Without Goals

Without goals,
a ship,
a plane,
a rocket,
or anything you can think of
would never reach its destination or its potential.

You see,
without goals,
we are all flying blind!

Window Shopping

Don't waste your time window shopping
for things you can't afford,
whether it's merchandise
or relationships.

Just be thankful for the things you have,
don't regret the things you don't have!!

Trust

It's important not to jump to conclusions.

Looks can be and often are, deceiving.

A person whom you have no interest
for when you first meet,
may turn out to be your perfect mate,
or someone you think is your friend
may be stabbing you in the back.

It is important for us not to be too friendly
or too cold with people,
until their behavior warrants it.

Keep an open mind,
but always remember...

Trust should never be given,
it must be earned.

Trust is like money.
If it is given to you, you are more likely to abuse it,
but if you earn it, you will use it more wisely.

Memorial Day

Every morning when I wake up,
the first thing I do
is thank God for all the blessings in my life.

But this morning is more important than others,
it is Memorial Day.

I hope everyone in this country takes the time
to thank God for the men and women who have
died to preserve this country's freedom,

Because if they had not fought
for what they believed in,
we would not be where we are today.

Outstanding Day

Everyday that you wake up
and you don't see your name in the obituaries,
you know it's going to be a good day.

And if it is a good day, why not go ahead and
make it an Outstanding Day?

Let's make today the day that we start living life
and stop letting life live us.

Take time to appreciate this precious gift called life,
and to realize that only you can make it outstanding.

Only you can decide that when you get out of bed
in the morning, you're going to get out on the right
side, have the right attitude, and live your life the
way it is meant to be…with passion, intensity,
effectiveness and power.

You can't impact anyone else
until you have made that change within yourself
that makes you outstanding.

Stop reacting, and start acting!

Take control of the situation, and if you do it with
enthusiasm and excitement, then you will see your
attitude will spread like wild fire.

Wardrobe of Vocabulary

Do you understand that your image is the first thing people see anywhere you go?

How important is it that we use this first impression to our advantage?

Look the look! Dress the part!

Show people who you are
before anyone
has to tell them!

Then, talk the talk!

Go through your wardrobe of vocabulary each morning and decide what words you are going to use.

The words that you use, and the passion and enthusiasm behind them are a major part of how people see you.

Make people stop and take notice.

Stand out by being outstanding!

Strive to be consistent in your positive image and you will see doors open that you never even knew existed.

Clear Focus and Clear Vision

My challenge to you today, is to set your sights,
and to strive toward hitting your goals.

Some of us may not have a clear focus
or a clear vision.

So ask yourself, "How do I do it?"

"How do I begin taking steps toward realizing
and achieving my dreams and goals?"

Use and enhance your own traits, gifts, and ability,
to create your dreams, and make them into tangible
goals, and visualize each step you can take to
achieve them.

Don't ask yourself, "What does it take?" Instead, ask
"What qualities do I have that will make this happen
for me?"

Use what God has given you naturally,
what makes you unique,
and you will be "outstanding!!"

The Longer I Live

The longer I live, the more I realize
the impact of attitude on life.

It's all attitude!

I am convinced that life is 10% of what happens to
me and 90% of how I react to it!

You know, people don't always understand me,
and I've seen that not everyone appreciates
enthusiastic people.

But I have decided, I will not let the things that
happen in my life determine my attitude, but rather,
I will let my attitude affect everything that happens
to me in my life!

Your attitude is the one and only thing you have
complete, 100% control over.

Think about it, and you'll realize that's all you've got!

Make the best of it, take advantage of it, and make
your attitude go to work for you!

"If you don't like the way you feel,
change the way you think!"

Understanding Courage

Courage is not a gift!

Courage is a decision!

Courage is not the absence of fear,
it is the presence of a calling . . .
A dream that pulls you beyond yourself.

Therefore, it is something you can never lose,
it is always something that you can choose.

So choose it today!

Just

I tell people all the time to take the word "just" out of their vocabulary.

Here is what I mean…

"I'm just a wife."

"I'm just a husband."

"I'm just a student."

"I'm just a truck driver."

"I'm just a sales person."

"I'm just a construction worker."

"I'm just an employee."

"I'm just a kid."

In all of these occupations,
the word "just" robs people
of the proper pride
they should have in their positions.

Outstanding People

It is no wonder how Outstanding People
make it in today's world.

They realize that low times are understandable
and sometimes even helpful.

What is most important is how we handle them.

What I am saying is,
to never make a negative decision
in a down time.

That is one time
when the decision not to make a decision
is a positive decision.

It proves that we are still in control of our moods.

Remember, the mood of a positive person
always returns.

Image

I   INSPIRE OTHERS!

M   MOTIVATE YOURSELF!

A   ASPIRE TO YOUR DREAMS!

G   GET OFF YOUR BUTT!

E   ENJOY THE REWARDS!

Focus

F Forget the Obstacles!

O Opportunity is Knocking!

C Come Answer the Door!

U Upset the Norm!

S Start Your Outstanding Life!

Who are Winners?

Who are winners?

What is a winner?

Winners are everyday heroes!

Winners take their dreams seriously!

Winners never give up and won't let you give up either!

Winners have outstanding attitudes!

Winners care in their sleep!

Winners make big things happen a little at a time!

Winners see the beginning in every ending!

Winners expect the best!

Time

I was walking through the airport.
I looked down at my shoes.

They were untied,
as I said to the Lord
I wish I had more time.

But you see, the memories started to roll by,
as I thought about all the people I had left behind.

Sitting there without a dime,
I started playing a game
just to take up some time.

They had "tic"
And I had "toe",
but just like my life,
they beat me 3 in a row.

It seems like all the good things are left behind.

What I am really saying, is that we don't take the
time
to find the little treasures in the people we leave
behind, and at that very second I made up my
mind to start to spend more time with all the people
I leave behind.

So be careful of the people you leave behind.

They may want just a little more of your time.

Just remember, be grateful for that four letter word,

"TIME."

Change

Change as a word is good, but every time you here the word "change," the person it's directed to is bad off.

You never hear someone who has just won the lottery complain about needing a change of luck,

NO, you hear phrases like "change of scenery" for someone who is in a bad relationship or "pitching change" when a baseball pitcher cannot get the "out" he or she needs.

So, when a loved one asks you to change, take these words to heart.

They may be giving you a clue about some way you can improve yourself.

Don't be so resistant to change, and try to be supportive when someone else is trying to change.

Like Rocky Balboa said, "Everyone can change."

Not Always Right

Today I'm going to tell you a Secret
that will make you feel a whole lot better
about yourself.

It's something you've allowed yourself
to consider before...
But not for very long.

The secret will make you tremble,
even though you know that accepting
it will ease your mind, calm your fears,
and even wet your appetite for growth.

Are you ready for it?
I know you can handle it.
Though not everyone can.

Well here it goes:

YOU ARE NOT ALWAYS RIGHT.

I saw you smile, because you know I'm right.

Trying to be right about everything
is a load you cannot carry.

The next time you look in the mirror,
you may want to remind yourself of this secret.

I'll tell you another secret, admitting that you're not
always right makes you even more loveable than
you already are, if that's possible.

Best Example

The best example of commitment
I have ever seen is Lance Armstrong.
He is the American cyclist
who overcame testicular cancer.
Not only did he defeat this disease,
but through his hard work, and persistence,
he won the Tour de France.

In case any of you are wondering,
that is the definition of commitment.
he not only won this race once,
he won it twice in a row,
and he is on the verge of winning his third.
I think everyone should strive
to have that kind of commitment.

Destination

Everybody knows somebody–
some of you might even be this person–
who dedicates themselves to improving their lives.
It might be going on a diet,
working out
or even taking on an academic course.
But about two weeks into their
new found challenge, they QUIT.
It has lost its novelty,
because they haven't seen any results.
This is where commitment has to take over.
With commitment
you'll have belief in what you're doing
and not look for the easy exit.
You'll find that with commitment,
the journey will be just as rewarding,
if not more, than the destination.

Anchors

Some peole are anchors.
No matter how good your idea is,
they tell you why it won't work
or why it can't be done.
They would rather sit in the mud
and slowly sink.
So, if you want to sail away to success,
then you have to cut the rope
off all your Anchors.

Win

There's an old saying,
"you can't win a race in the first lap,
but you can lose one."
This is very true,
the first lap leader of the Daytona 500
doesn't pull off the track
and on to victory lane.
No one remembers the leader
at the first lap
unless he is also the leader
at the last lap.
And even then,
only a few will remember it.
So, don't get discouraged
if you're not ahead right now.
Life is not a sprint,
it's a marathon
ANYONE CAN WIN!!

Commitment

Commitment isn't easy.
No decision ever is.
Just think about the last time you went to dinner.
How long did it take for you to decide
where to go and what to order?
This decision only affects your evening,
unless it's bad.
In that case
it could affect the next day too.
Commitment will affect your life,
so spend a little more time on this decision,
or you could end up with
more than just a stomach ache.

Cracker Jack Box

I've always believed
that no one ever really
outgrows a Cracker Jack Box.
At least not the surprise inside.

You know that the surprise doesn't amount to much.
Usually it is just some little plastic gadget,
but you still dig down inside the box
until you find out what kind of plastic gadget it is.
I think the same should hold true
of every person you meet
and everything you do.
There is some sort of surprise
inside each of us
and in everything we do.

This is John Dmytryszyn telling you
to see if you can find that hidden surprise,
just for the fun of it.

Think a Minute...

"What is the nicest thing
anyone's ever done for you?"

Maybe it was something your spouse
or your children
or a good friend
or neighbor
did for you that was particulary special.
Maybe it was a total stranger.

Today I ask you to think about it.
How did it make you feel?
Then take that feeling
and make someone else feel
that same way.

But

Everyone knows at least one person
who responds to every good suggestion
with the same two words,

Yeah, but...

Then comes any number of excuses.
You've heard them I'm sure.
It's too hard.
It's too simple.
There isn't enough time.
I'll do it later.
And so on and so forth.

What these people are saying
is that they're scared or just lazy.
They either want your help
or they want you to do it for them.
I'm here to tell you
that the way to help these kind of people
is to give them a swift kick in the ...

"Yeah, but!"

This is John Dmytryszyn telling you
that the procrastinator's club meeting
has been pushed back until tomorrow.

What If?

What if people never doubted themselves?
How would the world be different?
First of all, I would have to find another line of work.
But, on the good side,
there would be no indecision or regret.
Indecision causes hesitation and
he or she who hesitates is lost.
Regret comes from making the wrong decision,
not making a decision, or taking bad advice.
If the decision is yours,
then you know who to blame.
Self doubt is basically fear.
Fear to stand on your own without a crutch,
What if there were no crutches?
What if there was no fear?

This is John Dmytryszyn telling you
that as Winston Churchill said,
"The only thing we have to fear is fear itself."

Dare?

I'd rather be me than anyone else.
That's what I tell myself every day.
Don't waste your time
dreaming of having someone else's life.
If you're unhappy with your life,
Then only you can do something about it.
Dare to dream?
Dare to change?
Dare to live your own life?

...the OUTSTANDING life.

Tough Quality

Courage is a tough quality to come by.
Fear is everywhere.
People are constantly looking for courage.
CEOs will pay outrageous salaries for it.
But, you can't buy it.

Courage is quite simply the belief in your convictions,
combined with the certainty that you're right.
If you have the courage to believe in yourself,
it will wipe away your fear!

Sky's the LIMIT

When you're young,
you have your whole life in front of you.
You can do anything
when you're a kid.
As you get older
Your choices narrow
Well, guess what?
You start to believe
that you have limitations.
If you want to succeed,
you have to stop thinking like an adult
and start thinking like a CHILD.

I am here to tell you
the Sky's the LIMIT.

Greatness

"Some people are born with greatness,
and others have greatness thrust upon them!"

That's how the saying goes.
In my eyes,
there is nothing further from the truth.

Some of the biggest losers in life
have a great family name.
While others get their shot
and totally blow it.

Greatness is only achieved one way:
with hard work
and courage in your convictions!

News Flash

Here's a News Flash.
People are different!

Some people wake up
before their alarm sounds
and look forward to the day ahead.

Others hit the snooze button
and try to stay in bed.

Winners greet the day like it's a
new challenge to overcome
and losers roll over
and fall back to sleep.

Bullies

There was a girl named Jenny
Who was different from the rest.
She wanted to fit in
And tried her very best.

But some kids who were bullies
Were always very mean.
They hurt Jenny's feelings
And even more it seems.

Their words were very hurtful
Their actions made her blue
Why didn't they stop to realize
That Jenny had feelings too.

Jenny felt so lonely
It made her very sad
To think that people could be so cruel
It also made her mad.

Bullies may think they're funny
And cool to their friends
How would they feel with the tables turned
Their mean actions would soon end.

Every one of us is special
In his or her own way.
That's what we need to remember
Each and every day.

Pressure

Many times while I'm watching sporting events,
I can't help but think of the pressure
that the favorite is under.
Sure, both teams feel pressure to perform,
but if you're expected to win,
the pressure has to be multiplied.
Not only does everyone expect you to win,
they expect it to be relatively easy.
So the underdog's only job is to keep it close.
And the longer they keep it close,
the more pressure increases on the favorite.
Some teams, or people, can't deal with
that pressure, and they crumble.
If they can't handle the pressure and they choke,
eventually they will be the underdog
instead of the favorite.
Others relish it.
They're not afraid to say,
"I am better than you."
Then they let their play speak for itself.
Many people in society call these people
overconfident
and dislike their attitude.
But any betting man or woman
will tell you that nine out of ten times
the favorite wins, and they cover the spread.

21 Ways to Live The OUTSTANDING LIFE

Be forgiving

Trust your instincts

Be organized

Live with integrity

Be honest with yourself and others

Live with happy thoughts

Live to reach your goals

Know your true desire

Let your jealousies go

Live for yourself and then take care of others

Be confident

Have no boundaries

Enjoy your success

Be humble

Praise yourself

You become what you believe

Don't be afraid to ask for help

Have inner peace

Live with confidence

Accept a compliment

Let go of anger

Notes

Notes

Notes